THE WATCHMAN'S OPUS

A Poetry Compilation

Walter T. Lacy III

A.K.A Soul Emcee Detroit

Copyright 2020.

Walter T. Lacy III /Soul Emcee Detroit

Just Composition LLC

All rights reserved.

Published in the U.S.

No part of this book may be reproduced, in any form without expressed written permission from the publisher. If you would like to use material from the book (other than for review purposes), prior written consent must be obtained by contacting the publisher. Requests for permission should be e-mailed to justcomposition@gmail.com.

Acknowledgments

I must first acknowledge the Heavenly Father, for without the grace and blessings of the Most High, no good work is possible. I pray that the Lord sees this work and accepts it as an expression of love, compassion, atonement, and a lament for justice. I am an imperfect man, but my faith, and the love I have for my people is greater than my faults. I give praise and thanks for all that has been gifted to me. Through my creativity, and most importantly, by my character, I hope to fulfill my promise. Forgive me for my sins and shortcomings. Protect and keep me all my days.

Secondly, I acknowledge my family- blood and otherwise. Mama, I am forever grateful for your warmth, your humor, and the empathy you have for others. I might not care for people as deeply as I do, if not for the example that you and others have set. It is an honor to be your son. I am my mother's child, but I am my father's reflection. Pops, I give the utmost respect to you. I admire your resilience in overcoming the challenges you've faced (a trait you and Mama share). You find comedy in the struggle, imparting wisdom that only those who've fallen and gotten back up can provide. I remember the rhyming games we played when I was a child. I guess they're paying off now.

Sed, I appreciate you bro. I played rhyming games with my Pops, but I learned the art of emceeing from you. My love for Hip-Hop as a sound and culture was cultivated in a Freedom State basement. I don't take it for granted bro. One Love (Brothers Til' Da End). Doc Strange, I salute you. The teachings you've passed down over the years are invaluable. You are my uncle by blood, but in spirit, my second father. I thank you for being there all these years. Khalil: keep doing your thing. It is a blessing to see the young man you've become. Continue to set a dope example for your siblings. I see your focus and discipline. It inspires me to stay on point. Never lose your imagination or your spirit. Maintain your humility. Be a force for good. Shout out to the Lacys & the Johnsons; Freedom State & The Cypher extended family! To everyone that has had a hand in my development as an artist and as a man, thanks. I love y'all!

Author's Letter

Peace Family,

I pray that you receive the words expressed in this book with an open heart and mind. It is my hope that the perspective shared in these verses will stir your emotions in a way that draws you closer to the Most High, to your loved ones, and to the community you live in. I appreciate you for supporting this project. I look forward to building with you through the course of our respective journeys. May the light that lives in us be a flashlight amid the darkness of the world we live in. LOVE & RESPECT 2 YOU ALWAYS!

                                        Walter T. Lacy III, A.K.A Soul Emcee Detroit

For the Poets & Emcees

Those who rock on stages. Those who write their stories.

For the listeners and the readers.

For the thinkers, the dreamers, & the teachers.

For the people of faith. For those that pursue justice.

For those just trying to make it.

For our young people- don't give up on joy, or

your potential to achieve something great.

For Detroit.

For you, wherever you are.

Love now & Always.

~Dedication~

VERSES

Op. No. 1: The Hits Keep Coming (p. 1)

Op. No. 2: A Conversation Between Revolutionaries (p. 5)

Op. No. 3: Afraid of Shadows (p. 7)

Op. No. 4: Enemy of the State (p. 10)

Op. No. 5: Rabbit Hole (p. 12)

Op. No. 6: Sledgehammer (p. 16)

*Op. No. 7: Line of Scrimmage (p. 19)

Op. No. 8: False Religion (p. 22)

Op. No. 9: Matador (p. 25)

*Op. No. 10: Timeless [A Tribe Called Us] (p. 27)

Op. No. 11: Public Transportation (p. 31)

Op. No. 12: These Streets Talk (p. 35)

Op. No. 13: Eye Shadow (p. 38)

Op. No. 14: You Are Not "Pretty" (p. 42)

Op. No. 15: Discipline (p.45)

Op. No. 16: You Are Not Invisible (p. 48)

Op. No. 17: Master Mold (p. 50)

Op. No. 18: Come the Apocalypse (p.52)

Op. No. 19: The Resonance of Silent Weapons (p.54)

Op. No. 20: Endure (p. 57)

Op. No. 21: When the Music Stops (p. 60)

Op. No. 22: To Love a Stranger from Afar (p.63)

Op. No. 23: After Mourning (p. 65)

Op. No. 24: Oasis (p. 68)

Op. No. 25: Masquerade (p. 70)

Op. No. 26: Call & Response [By the Blind No More] (p. 73)

Op. No. 27: The Watchman's Opus (p. 77)

Op. No. 28: Play My Music Loud (p. 81)

Line of Scrimmage originally published in INSIGHT by FOKUS: "Borders" December 2018

Timeless originally published in INSIGHT by FOKUS: "Tribe" December 2017

THE WATCHMAN'S OPUS

The Hits Keep Coming

Marvelous Motor City,
Rhythmic sound of concrete jungle soul.
I listen to your melodies with open ears.
Receive your love with open arms,
Though at times, that love is hard to come by.

We are graduates of the school of hard knocks here.
Overtime grind, 9 to 5 hours after your shift was supposed to end.
But we punch the clock, and keep working here.
Punch your lights out for ever doubting the depth of our resolve.
It is unwise to question our mettle, or to test our spirit.

From "The Brown Bomber" to "The Hitman,"
We are a city of world champions.
Emanuel Steward getting crunk at Kronk's Gym,
This is a city that builds character.
We are trained fighters here.

Not just survivors, but those that thrive by sheer will of faith.
We are the rough edges,
At times, hard-headed.
But we are still people who believe in God here.

From sweet hearted mamacitas that greet you at
Honeybee Market,
Where Auntie Joyce and Uncle Pete cop tortillas.
Get just the right spices, before they cook the corned beef
For another birthday edition of ghetto bingo.

To hood scholars that rock hoodies like Tony Stark's armor;
Speaking the language of hustlers raised on volatile street corners.

But never disrespect the elders.
They pay homage to those who came before us.

It's no wonder why mama fed my homeboys as if they were her own sons.
Family dinners became celebrations.
Celebrations became block parties that brought together the whole neighborhood.
I tip my hat to Freedom State,
A place where I came to know myself at an early age.
One of many precious gems that you can find here.

This beautiful city- where diamonds are mined on blacktop.
Leather plucks the netted chords,
We play string music all night long.
Cue the *Iceman*, smooth as a finger roll.

We are the Bad Boys who upset the status quo,
Passed the torch to go to work.
Mr. Big Shot, Sheed, and Rip.
The Palace Prince and Fear the Fro.
Fight the powers that be, too much like Hollywood for me.
Tap. Tap.
Rick Mahorn, Laimbeer, and the Worm.
A city of two captains that captured
Larry and Stanley's thrones.

Home of Zeke & Stevie Y,
Rock city. Hockeytown.
Overtime. Grind Line.
We sacrifice our bodies.
Give blood, sweat, and jabs, just for a chance to shine.

The hits keep coming.
Like The Jackson 5, when the

King of Pop was just little Michael with the afro.

The hits keep coming.
A humble running back from Kansas,
By way of Stillwater, Oklahoma.
Ran for 2,000 yards, Most Valuable Player, and a
Playoff spot at the Silverdome.

The hits keep coming.
A humble wide receiver from Georgia Tech,
Breaking Jerry Rice's records.
Such a beast that he became a Transformer:
Megatron.

The hits keep coming.
Before punk rock was punk rock.
The Hackney brothers breathed life into music as a
Band called Death.

The hits keep coming.
From *Let's Get it On* to *What's Going On?*
Marvin Gaye sang ballads that resonate as anthems still today.

The hits keep coming.
From the Queen of Soul,
R E S P E C T is earned, to
Martha Reeves and the Vandellas who brought the heat wave on, for the
Long hot summers that were soon to follow.

And the hits keep coming.

We are a city of *temptations and miracles*.
Woeful sinners reborn as righteous instruments.

Harpsichords, church organs, electric guitars majestically harsh.
Boom bap, heavy bass, synthesizer, soul samples.
Word to J Dilla.

Poetic ramblings, exquisite masterpieces.
We are the masterpiece: a puzzle of stories untold,
Just waiting to be heard.
We are the D.
Motown.
The Motor City.
I'm from Hitsville.
Where the hits just keep on coming.

A Conversation between Revolutionaries

-For the poets, the emcees, the thinkers, and believers.

CAUTION.

The space that you have entered is neither for the weak at heart, nor for the fragile minded.

It is a breeding ground for visionaries.

Instruments of freedom songs in the face of fascist war drums.

We are one nation.

Not divided by border patrol agents policing stolen acres to nullify the agency of

My tribal ancestors.

We are not slaves to their occupation.

I attest; that we are servants of a divine presence.

Reflected in the passionate tone of our speech, a

Thunderous roar rumbling against the backdrop of a boom-bap.

Let us speak: to one another in the language of

Follow the Drinking Gourd.

It is the souls of young warrior poets & prophets that will light the way North,

For Heaven is but an intimate verse away.

We are messengers.

Heralds of Revelation for a world on the brink of destruction,

Needing transformation.

Let us seize this moment to speak the truth.

Mobilized by a common gift and purpose,

Let us raise our voices to shake the chains of desperation &

Breathe new life into our people.

For if this world dies away,

The memories we've made and the

Love that we've shared will

Transcend time.

Let us cultivate a movement.

A conversation between revolutionaries.

It won't end merely with words.

Afraid of Shadows

The boogeyman still lurks beneath the beds of
Policemen who are too petrified to fulfill their oaths.
Perhaps not all of them are yellow.
Maybe, they aren't all spineless.
But it seems, to me at least,
That there are too many licensed killers with shaky fingers.
Poorly trained, awfully timid, often fear-stricken,
Cowardly agents stealing a paycheck as they continue to remain on
City payroll.

I find it hard to be mere coincidence;
America's prisons filled with the progeny of those
Once considered three-fifths of a citizen.
Hard labor without pay or death,
The preferred sentence for being found guilty of a crime.

Thin is the line that exists between
Slave patrols, night watchmen, overseer, and officer.
Slavery has been legal since America's inception.
An endless thread of nightmarish dreams weaving through history.
Across time- there is no space.
Nowhere is it safe to be Black in this treacherous nation.

Not even in a city as rich as mine.
85% Black- a chocolate paradise at times.
A small slice of heaven amidst these hellish confines.
A haven for southern migrants, like our
Big mamas and grandfathers coming from
Alabama, Mississippi, and Tennessee.

Left the fields to manufacture.

From the plantation to the plant.
In search of better days,
Our people sweat about the same for a little extra pay.
Just a little bit more stable, until they
Railroaded our neighborhoods,
Destroying them to build freeways.

In memory of Blackbottom.

Generations of Black folks scraping the bottom of overrun ghettos.
Left to die on streets named after leaders that
Never lived long enough to see the revolution be televised.
So, here we are.
Mourning the loss of enemies of the State;
Black faces erased by bastards with badges, or
Self-righteous zealots, who fashion themselves as
Upstanding vigilantes.

With tears in our eyes, we lament for salvation.
Pray for the family of Malice Green.
Though he was beaten to death years ago,
We still remember him.

For Brandon Martell Moore;
A 16 year-old gunned down from behind.
He died by the barrel of a sambo's gun.
A Black man so enamoured with white supremacy,
He must've believed his uniform was an opportunity to
Change his skin tone.

For every Walter Budzyn, Larry Nevers, or
Fill-in-the-blank with more infamous white racist's name,
There's an empty shell of a Eugene Williams, or an Olivia Pope type figure, who will

Dance as a puppet on a string, to have a taste of American Pie.

Neck-rolling judas in a druid's robe.
Cynthia Gray Hathaway;
You are no righteous judge, only a wretched pawn.
Refusing to even prosecute Aiyana's killer for manslaughter.
He should've been sentenced to prison for murder.
You the *coach, the quarterback, and the owner.*
Indignant, filled with pride and self-hatred.
How dare you boast your title in the face of a family and community
That had to bury one of its daughters?

The old heads say that these young folks lost.
If that's the case, then who's at fault?
For years we've played their political games,
While we're still being lynched in the streets today.
We move ever closer to the point of not taking it anymore, to the
Point of taking the justice that we seek by force.

The beatings. The killings. The corruption. The cover-ups.
Their municipal military does not protect or serve us.
We live our days under a microscope that doubles as crosshairs.
While they shoot to kill, ask questions later.
Cry wolf, play the victim, then plead for forgiveness.
The law & order, considered armed & dangerous.
But nonetheless, afraid of shadows.

Enemy of the State

~For victims & survivors of the school-to-prison pipeline

I refuse to pledge allegiance to your flag.
I owe no loyalty to you this morning.
I've seen my loved ones lose their lives in your wars, but
I am treated like an inmate in this nation of *ours*.
A nation built by hands like mine, on
Broad shouldered backs cut by leather hide.
No chains, no chains, no chains on me.
But still I walk these lands unfree.
Unfree to live. Unfree to learn.

Is it still illegal for me to read?
I'm behind these walls for knowledge's sake.
But you don't teach, you just oversee.
You're here to control, to dominate me.

In grand suburbs does it look like this?
No chance in hell. This is ghetto shit.

A wisecrack. A scuffle. An immature joke.
No reason for the system to jump down my throat.
For my pops to be angry.
For mama's disappointment.

For my teacher's disdain in a class I don't want.
A class I don't need.
A class I don't need.
It's remedial work to the genius in me.

You pat me down. Take my money and my phone.
But won't provide me with books. Suspend me.
Then send me home.
Now I'm out too early.
Citation for truancy.
Falsely accused, fit the description.
10-15 for assault and armed robbery.

Behind these walls for knowledge's sake.
The knowledge I seek. The knowledge you take.
Put me in a cage, so that you can feel safe.
I am not your criminal.
I am not a mistake.
I am the reminder of your demons.

Public Enemy of the State.

Rabbit Hole

We are more free than we've been led to believe, though the
Myths we've learned make this
Earth less paradise,
More penitentiary.
Solitary confinement.
Entrapped by concrete isolation.
Not constrained with bars,
Instead by fears, condemned by faults.
Those thoughts that echo boisterously,
Above the quiet peace that we seek.

Unable to silence the noise of fruitless conversations
With friends and family members that have been
Terribly mislead,
As they regurgitate ideals from the network on
Their side of the aisleway.

The beliefs and actions of every man, woman, and child,
Micro-managed & artificially implanted.
From cradle to grave, thoughts disseminated by a
Slim fraction of individuals with a vested interest in
Creating dysfunction.
In order to assure their reign, beyond the scope of television ratings.

Peel the layers back.
Grab your shovel.
Strike the ground right here where the bullshit is fresh.
Start digging.
In the same spot where
Lola Bunny lays her easter eggs.
Let us see how funny this tragedy gets as we
Tumble down the rabbit hole. (We are subjects for)
A social experiment that has gone terribly wrong.
It seems humankind is at the point of
Collectively losing its sanity.
Suffering the shared experience of
Trauma-based mind control.

Fed image after dreadful image,
Filled with terror.
Left with an unhealthy numbness,
Unshakeable haunting.
Ghosts imbedded in our psyche, like
Journalists paid to lie about the horrors of
America's war machine.
This unholy land of hypocrisy; where
Kneeling in protest of a flag that symbolizes the
Hatred, enslavement, and exploitation of my people is

Branded as treasonous.
Yet, sacrificing our future for their petroleum and opium;
Giving life and limb for unrighteous puppets who
Sanction unjustified imperialist invasions and genocides is
Lauded as patriotism.

Our reality transcends party affiliations.
Ballot boxes will not unlock the doors to liberty.
Only concessions made to bring about compromise, as we come to
Accept the illusion that is the lesser of two evils.

Donald Trump bullhorns a push to build his border wall.
Close the shores to refugees that flee the aftermath of Obama's drones;
A product of the Bush and Clinton wars.
Barbarians posing as statesman,
More aptly described as pawns playing dress up in
Kings' robes.

They are living proof that our fight is not
Against flesh and blood alone,
But those that move in shadows trying to overthrow the
Almighty God.

Forgive me for my missteps.
None of us are absolved from sin.

Even still, let me stand for the oppressed,
Shed light upon this world's deceptions.
3 buildings imploded on 9/11.
What happened to World Trade Center 7?
Did anyone listen to Benazir Bhutto before she was assassinated?
Was bin Laden dead before the May Day-Beltane ritual slaying?

I don't know the answers to these things.
I simply pose the question- yes,
I know what
I believe, so
I change the channel frequently.
Change the channel frequently.
Tune to a different frequency.

I am free.
Don't tell me otherwise.
I think for me.
Don't tell me otherwise.
I am flawed, but I am not lost.
We are more than we've been taught.
Sometimes it just takes a
Trip down the rabbit hole, to find out
Exactly who we are.

Sledgehammer

I pray for a sledgehammer,
Molded by the Creator's hand.
Shaped from the molten metal of
Mother Earth's volcanoes.
A purifying flame that welds the hammerhead to the strongest redwood.
Justice written about its handle in seven different languages.
Etched into stone: branded by the sound of thunder to authenticate the
Most High's signature.

The world cannot continue in this fashion.
Indiscriminate killing and blasphemous indignities.
Children of the world suffer without food, shelter, and water.
Nations are placed under sanctions as America plays policemen for
The entire world.
Leveraging political angles to exert control over the geopolitical landscape.
A life & death game of chess taking place on a war room ouija board.

Iron fist brought down on the heads of her enemies: humanity.
Beating democracy into our brains in an attempt to wash away our rationale, that we
Fail to call America's brand of governance by its name:
Fascism.

Don't speak to me about a post-racial society.

Not when Renisha McBride can have her face blown off for wearing the wrong skin color, as
She stumbled to the wrong white man's door in need of assistance.
Not when Eric Garner is rushed by the NYPD:
Choked to death for declaring his right to live as a free human being.
Whether or not he was selling loosies.
It does not make a difference to me.

Don't talk to me about how great Barack Obama is.

Not when he has authorized more drone strikes than George W. Bush did.
Not when he insults my intelligence as he professes "Israel's" right to defend itself.
Justifying the genocide of Palestinians that began in 1948 and has escalated.
We are at the threshold of World War III.
Maybe, it has already begun, but we are too blind to see it.
Perhaps our vision has been clouded by chemicals used for cloud seeding.
Our thoughts disrupted by waves of energy blasted into the sky, as
We are tuned to hear the synthetic notes of fallen angels on their HAARP.

We have learned to mute the desperate groans of
Wailing parents whose sons and daughters are murdered by
Hellfire missiles.
Learned to hush the cries of little boys and girls
Molested by people that they thought loved them; by
Religious figures they trusted.
Vicars who attempt to play God, but no one holds them accountable.

The pope just asks for forgiveness.

He is not holiness, but everything that is unholy.
A spiritual lynchpin for occult lynching.
The people have become sacrificial lambs amidst a biblical slaughterhouse.
The clock is ticking.
We inch closer to nuclear holocaust or digital panopticon.
Enslaved by the luxury of machines we've been trained to love more than
Human beings.

Freedom requires us to evolve.
We can no longer afford to ignore its call.
For inner-city youth slain by guns every day.

For child soldiers and victims of the sex-slave industry.
For little girls kidnapped by Boko Haram.
For Iraqis still suffering after Saddam.
I pray for a sledgehammer from the hand of God, to
Break the chains of oppression, the will of tyrants, and
Bring about justice in an unjust time.

Line of Scrimmage

I grew up in a townhouse apartment complex surrounded by metal fences.
I am convinced that this was no coincidence.
I give thanks for learning the depth of irony so young.
Born & raised in Freedom Place.
We OSB's call it Freedom State.
Free is a place I've sought for years
But a state that is hard to achieve,
When the bars around your home,
Mimic the walls that consume our brethren.

Prisoners of war in a fight between good vs. evil.
Exorcising the demons that seek to destroy us from within
Whilst fighting d'evils that aim to eradicate our people.
Poisonous pigs with a license to kill.
The self-righteous cowards who murdered Tamir.
CIA henchmen with a penchant for violence.
Black operations.
Assassinations, coup d'etats, and
Black market politics.

Parlor tricks mastered by sleight of hand.
Mass manipulation from media mouthpieces,
Mobilized to orchestrate madness.
Order sustained through organized chaos.
Society walks a tightrope along the edge of insanity.
Who knows what awaits when the line of scrimmage is passed.

As border patrol agents unload tear gas canisters at migrant caravans,
Like riot police trying to impose their will upon
Protesters who sought justice in Ferguson.
In Baltimore.

At Standing Rock.

The foundations of humanity have been shaken in such a way,
That human beings are hardly recognizable.
Men and women have become more like automatons,
Than spirits of free will and critical thought
Made in the image of God.

Our existence is deeper than campaign promises made to conceal hidden agendas.
Masks worn by politicians that marvel us with charisma,
Only to cloak their true intentions,
before twisting the dagger into our collective spinal cord.
A psychic unity short-circuited by the illusion of choice.
Donald trumpets the alarms of racist fear-mongering.
Persistent in his efforts to construct a wall that will stand as
A monument to America's decline.

A revelation of deceit, that belies its stated commitment to the cause of liberty.
No refuge for refugees in pursuit of happiness, who would settle for survival.
Those who pray for asylum in the aftermath of Obama's bombs,
A continuation of the Bush and Clinton families' war on fill-in-the-blank.
Not to mention that many immigrants are fleeing from nations broken
By Bill & George's free trade agreements.

But I digress.
In short, the suffering of others is hard to digest.
As disgusting as Nike knighting Colin Kaepernick
To become a Black face for Phil Knight's white hypocrisy.
There was no concern for morality or human rights
When his workers were living on less than a dollar a day.
Being beaten and killed for protesting their pay.
Given a half-ass apology, some settlement money, and a minimal increase in wages.
But the machine keeps moving.

Parlor tricks mastered by sleight of hand.
Order sustained through organized chaos.
Who knows what awaits when the line of scrimmage is passed.
Eventually, we will all have to decide whether we will
Stay on-side or cross the line of scrimmage.
But once you jump offsides,
There is nowhere to go, but forward.
And no safe space out of bounds.

False Religion

We live in the age of false religion.
A day where human beings are no longer spiritual entities.
Mankind has been reduced to energy.
Input. Output.
It is simple. We are batteries.
Dehumanized, commoditized, quantified.
Inventory checked and tracked
Under the watchful gaze of a technocratic security state.
Tentacles stretching across the Earth to squeeze the life out of dying souls.

From satellites that beam
Nightmares into your dreams.
Destruction, depravity.
Decadence, insanity.
The masses made dumb,
Incapable of interpreting the insults hurled at our intelligence.

From basketball games played on aircraft carriers, to
Super Bowl flyovers that foster pseudo patriotic emotions.
Stealth bombers and attack choppers profiled for your evening news coverage.
We are bombarded with symbols that appeal to imperialist ideals.
Displays to the world that might is righteous.

We are spoken to as babies.
A herd of shepherdless sheep, driven to the front lines of immoral wars.
Stratified into right-left paradigms that create controlled opposition for
Synthetic conflicts.
Immersed in the rat race, we chase validation.
Distinction defined by $ signs.
From business executives to low-level dope boys,
Both waving the flag for team America.

Therein the problem exists.
My kinfolks are displaced descendants of chosen people stripped of their identity.
Ethiopian blood set ablaze by sunlight at the epicenter of creation.
Hebrews that knew the Creator before
Greeks and Romans hijacked the image of our faith;
Changing its face, its purpose, and its name.
Now our people are at odds over fiat currency.
That means we feud over money that is worthless.
Fight tooth-and-nail for *in God we Trust,*
Become contortionists to get a seat at tables for the wicked.
But don't serve the poor or fight against injustice.

Boastful of accolades,
A society that celebrates its status
With endless status updates.
Consumed with a culture of celebrity,
Basking in the relative poverty that defines
Ghetto super-stardom: we 'hood rich.

Material gain succumbs to living above your means.
Achievement, title, and salary lead to vanity & hubris.
Doing alright for yourself,
Affirmed as exactly that,
Until the timeless hammer
Called reap what you sow
Rears its head, and
You find out that you're alone, or worse:
Bound to a character portrayed to fulfill the needs of unseen owners.

There is no Heaven for unrepentant sinners.
No freedom on this Earth for the selfish & self-obsessed.
Ain't no perfection in this world.

But if we care about each other,
Account for where we've fallen short
There's hope for the future to produce more than the trappings of
Idol worship.

Matador

What happens when the bull becomes a matador?
A ninjutsu warrior, laser-focused
Trained at the feet of his
Elders, for the sole purpose of
Slaying conquistadors.
Eyes bloodshot, but not with rage.
Instead, something far more dangerous.

Precise in his vision,
Total balance of body and spirit.
In harmony with himself,
The hunted, no longer.
A ruler of his domain,
He is an unbound slave.
Call him MASTER.

A teacher for generations too expansive to calculate.
Feet that have walked the soil of this Earth, for
More lifetimes than the number of stars that light the
Firmament at night.

He is eternal.

A still breeze that whips around the sands in an arena.
Ominous calm before the proverbial storm.
Horns that pierce the sides of his enemies like
The spear that wounded the Messiah.
But they are not Martyrs.

They are generations of discord,
Agents of malice.

Those that kill for thrills,
Blood spilled to fill oceans.
Plague upon Earth, which has left the lands barren.
Sterilized by bitter waters,
But they are no match for him.

Their adornments, gold & silver,
are merely shiny.
They fail to capture the majesty of the bull as he is.
Unchained. Unbowed.
Not for your amusement.
Not for a twisted sacrifice.
The spirit of the Creator moves through him.
Feel the Earth tremble!
Stampede. Heartbeat.
The sound, THUNDER!
Smashing the pillars that keep your coliseums upright.
Let them crumble under foot.
Go the way of ancient empires turned to ashes.
Set aflame by the fire in his eyes,
That he and his tribe may roam free.

No one will bleed him, nor chase him.
Understanding that you can not run with a
Matador.

Timeless (A Tribe Called Us)

Only fools fail to count their blessings, and
Not many things measure up to the gift of family.
Genuine bonds are not easily broken.
They endure the trials of conflict,
Withstand the burden of grief, and overcome
Collective shortcomings to stand tall in the face of adversity.

I say family, with an understanding that such love is
Not exclusive to blood relation.
My kinship extends beyond borders,
Transcends the racial lines that divide us,
Despite an innate distrust for most white folks.

The world can be a lonely place sometimes,
Yet, I find camaraderie in those who write dope rhymes.
Relative unknowns cutting their teeth in freestyle sessions;
On street corners & college campuses.
Mastering the intricacies of soliloquy and beatnik poems.

Heart to hearts often shared on stage, for
Nameless faces that respect what you do,
But are mostly there to be entertained.
Not to feel the pain that emanates from your

Voice as it bellows, to shake the foundations of the
Heavens and Earth.

I watch the suffering of my people as mankind
Sinks further into a treacherous abyss of its own creation.
Libyans held at gunpoint, barrel to temple
As the stories of old manifest before our eyes.
And a lost generation bears witness to the horrors of slavery.

How do we find our soul?

Listen to the music of young children whose imaginations
Run free with visions of superheroes.
Turning the pages of comic books for inspiration, which often shatters the illusions of hopelessness
That chokes the life out of adults.
The babies see truth above all else, but are not oblivious to the differences that make us
Question our existence.
Wisdom lies in innocence.
Eyes that analyze character, more than superficial symbols.

I give thanks for the ones I call fam.
Genuine bonds are not easily broken.
Fortified by fist fights, football games, and life in public housing.
Harassed by narcs, lurking the hood for low-level pushers.

Long days, that became all-nighters writing essays for classes I cared nothing about.
Vibing with emcees and singers, that fed my spirit
Like Mama's prayers and Michigan Wolverines' victories.
Reminiscing on yesterday like the old heads bumping
Frankie Beverly & Maze.

We Are One.

Some chosen by blood, others by circumstance.
But all in accord with a Creator who loves us.
Otherwise, I wouldn't know *you*.
Brothers from other mothers that wax poetically on video games,
Beautiful dames, music, philosophy, and anime.
Splendid sisters with righteous fists raised from
Detroit to Houston. Oakland to New York.
Afros that bask in the glory of the sun.
Nappy-haired ponytails complimenting
Complex intellect and dangerous curves,
On standby for revolution.

For you, I pen words to pages.
A charge to act, and a dedication.
We ain't dead yet, so live my baby.
Sip the waters of resistance, but

Don't forget to dance like nobody's watching.

Lift your sword & shield for justice,

But don't hesitate to hug somebody.

We Are One.

Connected. Eternal. Timeless.

A Tribe Called

Us.

Public Transportation

Breathe deeply before you face the day's mission.
Nothing is promised or guaranteed.
Nobody owes you anything.
Give thanks.

Smell the fresh aroma of fireworks, or is it gunsmoke?
Permeating the clouds that tower above us common folks,
Just trying to make our way from
One place to another.

I pace myself steadily from the front door to the
Intersection of 6 Mile & Livernois.
Got four options to choose from, depending on which direction
I want to travel.

I usually take the 16 Dexter bus or 29 Linwood as I set out to
Handle business like an artist who has no intention of starving.
Early mornings up against bitter cold,
Designed to strip the will from one's soul.
But Detroiters don't fold so easily.
I keep it moving.

Hoodie on under my winter coat as an
Arctic chill descends upon Michigan.
I still gotta get to Ypsilanti.
There are kids- some of them from my city,
All of them extended family.
They expect me to be in for work, so that
We can wax poetic and free ourselves through verse.

They teach as much as they learn.

A constant reminder of why I picked up my pen in the first place.
So I stand,
Waiting for that Dexter bus, so that I can make it to the
Amtrak Station.
I put my headphones in.
Listen to an old CD player with
Dope instrumentals blaring to mix the paint that
Moves inside my brain, so that I'm prepared when it's
Time to use my brush.

I breathe deeply.
Listen to the old heads speak about yesteryear
As if it was yesterday.
Vivid memories that recall triumphs, sorrows, hellos, so longs,
Speakeasies, drug dealers, bootleggers, gangsters, fiends, hos, and pimps.

It's not uncommon to hear a conversation or two about politics.
People still waiting for the revolution.
I pray that it starts within.
Young brothers barely old enough to grow peach fuzz,
Talking 'bout how many chicks they hit.
Young sisters posture, playing tough.
Talking money, and who ass they gon' kick.

The cycle continues for the next hood nigga, or
Boss ass bitch, but don't condemn these babies,
It didn't start with them.
Perhaps a system that builds prisons to replace the
Schools that failed them.
Not to mention, they must digest the madness
Relentlessly fed to them.
Synthetically modified foolishness to
Convince us that we are not worthy.

Sometimes the youth move in silence.
Keep order amongst themselves,
Fully aware not to cuss around the elders,
Even when the old folks talk to themselves.
Curse everybody around them, or perhaps no one.
It's a constant battle to maintain our mental health.

I hear conversations about why the Lions need a new quarterback,
No matter how well he plays.
I hear dreams and realities.
See hope and despair.
Feel the excitement of the day, the
Exhaustion of the night.
Smell the fresh aroma of scented oils, or is it weed smoke?

Watch the driver pull over to
Run into the gas station to grab a Faygo.
Run into Little Caesars, for a hot 'n' ready,
McDonald's, for a McDouble.
Look out the window on the 29, see the young brothers hooping.
Little girls playing double-dutch.

Look at Central High School's football field,
Remember my cousin Demond running a kick return back for a touchdown,
As I pass Boston-Edison in the summertime.
Think about a Boston Cooler from the Dairy Queen,
No, I mean Dairy Whip, nearby.
Not far from my ex-girlfriend's house.
How I miss the good times, but time passed us by.

Take the loop around Zone 8.
I hope that my homie Donecia's people are good.
Let me off at Warren & Trumbull though, so I can kick it with Pops.

Listen to Jimi Hendrix, a lot of Prince, a little bit of Kraftwerk.
Get a few snacks from University
Eat, laugh, reflect.
Get up in time to catch my bus.

Get home, rest my hat;
Wake up. Breathe deeply.
Nobody owes me anything,
But y'all continue to give me everything.

I give thanks.

These Streets Talk
*For Cass Corridor, Southwest Detroit, & Dearborn
-with acknowledgement to Steve Nealing, Motor City Muckraker Investigative Journalist
& Donald Goines, Author "Black Girl Lost"

Get in the house when the streetlights come on!
No one knows what awaits when darkness falls.
When the sun gives way to a dense, thick fog;
When the air smells ripe with the scent of lit blunts.
Hustlers pound the pavement,
Chucking cigarettes butts in the street that often
Disappear into manhole covers.

Pimps peddling pain as pleasure
Lurk in the cover of night that
Fails to hide the sins of
Cass Corridor.
Where bombshells in bop-tail dresses were
Turned on by players in pink gators, rollin' in old-school
Cadillacs coated in candy paint,
Glazed with a fresh wood-grain interior.

Turned out by heavy-handed pusher men, who
Turned into vampires once their masks were off.
They fed on the flesh of Black girls lost to life in the fastlane.
Fast cars.
Fast money.
Quick fixes.
Take a hit of this shit right here will get you lifted,
If it doesn't kill you.

Take you to heights only reached by the
Unmarked military planes that brought us the heroin and crack cocaine.

This is pure.

Like a guilt-ridden Vietnam veteran,
Haunted by images of the
Children he assaulted.
Those melted by napalm, poisoned by
Agent orange.
Unable to shake his nightmares,
He sits alone in the Old Miami
Drinking whiskey as if it was holy water, to
Cleanse himself of all that he had done.

These streets be talking.

Like the strip on Michigan Avenue, where
Strip clubs and good food are familiar, but
Not more than ICE & border patrol agents
Running surveillance through
Southwest Detroit's neighborhoods.
"Homeland security" from there to Dearborn.
What a shame that they oppress more than they secure anything.

Supposedly, they run drug raids to obtain contraband, and
Detain alleged gangbangers.
Checkpoint; show your papers when they invade the mosque.
As adherents to Islam give their praises in Arabic.

The FBI gunned down
Imam Luqman Ameen Abdullah in a Detroit warehouse.
He was shot 21 times, but they accused him of being
Radical.
I question, where is the passionate call for justice?

Young kids go missing,
Men and women are led to slaughter.
Left upon the wretched altars of
Politicians and businessmen, who beat the table about the
Plague of crime or terrorism,
Then plunge their filthy hands into every racket from
Gambling to no-bid contracts;
School-to-prison pipeline for profits, and sex-trafficking.

These streets be talking.

No posh restaurants for hipsters will erase the memories lived here.
Good, bad, or indifferent,
We deal with reality here.

Swank lofts built to price out the former tenants.
Homeless citizens made invisible for special events;
Robbed by cops, kidnapped and driven out beyond the city limits.

Brainard Hills Park.
Taken care of by the people of Cass Corridor for years, was
Padlocked to keep them out of it.

A place of celebration, a testament to the heart of this city.
Barbecues. Basketball games. Graduations.
Moments that will last a lifetime,
Sold out for a parking lot.
Hear the echoes.
Understand that they are not ghosts.
These streets live.
These streets breathe.
These streets talk.
We better listen to them.

Eye Shadow

Forgive me Lord, for I am nothing more than a man.
I have fallen short of faultlessness, yet by your mercy
I continue to stand.
Imperfect at best,
A flawed and human being,
Yearning freedom, while seeking satisfaction.
They weigh upon my thoughts simultaneously.

She whispers when she speaks to me.
A temptress in a red jersey-dress,
Cut from leather and latex,
Lips wet with anticipation
Thighs spread for lust,
Eyes shadowed to block the light that
Might undo her disguise.

They call her by many names.
Harlot. Slut. Vixen. Whore.
Perhaps she is due the price of shame,
But what hypocrites are we that bear witness to her debasement?
Amuse ourselves in her descent,
Dismissed as mindless entertainment.

We are the products of a sex-crazed generation,
Entrenched in the woes of a Godless nation.
Seduced by her, brickhouse built like Amazon.
Fallen angel cast out from Heaven,
Left to fall upon casting couch;
Ensnared by hollywood's tendrils,
An unholy hell on Earth.

Swayed by the allure of fame,
Entombed by isolation
Broken and trained like a thoroughbred mare
She rides hung stallions and bucks
Until her eyes roll back into her head,
And her spirit dies along with theirs
As they fall back in time together,
Shackled and prone by the
Stocks outside the slave cabins.

Tears run down her face.
Lips wet. She anticipates him.
Shaken with fear,
Thighs spread for lust,
Eyes shadowed to block the light,

That might reveal the truth behind her cries.
They call her by many names.
Jezebel. Prostitute. Hottentot.
Daughter.
We must remember,
She was an innocent child, before
She became a disreputable woman.

Forced to grow up fast.
Left in the streets for dead.
Passed around from abuser to abuser,
As she moved through foster care.
Molested by papa, deceived by Prada.
She becomes a private dancer,
Branded and sold as black market product.

Shame on me for sitting back and watching.
Shame on those who turn depravity into profit.
Shame on the churches and power brokers that
Protect their codes of silence; who hush the alarms
As young starlets are sacrificed and
Turned into sirens.

I see her clearly now.

Not the temptress I assumed her to be.

But the soul of a young girl whispering,

"Father, give me peace"

Tortured by the violence she's seen,

Behind the shadowed eyes of a disreputable woman.

You are Not "Pretty"

Dear Black woman,
You are not pretty.

You are not pretty for a dark-skinned girl.

You are an unspoken truth that defies
Eurocentric standards of beauty.

Midnight sky, stars shining against moonlit obsidian
Dark-chocolate perfection dipped in molten marinade
Sun-baked tiramisu mocha-glazed

Your skin echoes the wisdom of distant memories.
Sankofa songs spoken in parables to impart knowledge to the young.
It is deliberately ignored, or written out of history that
You are mother to us all.

Eloquent genius singing our freedom into being;
Nina Simone, calling us to
Embrace the blackness in our souls as divine synergy.
Your daughters are shaded in an array of
Melanin bliss.

A modern-day griot
Determined to Excel in Everything Promised;
A PhD graduate in computer science from an institution where
The Black woman's mind is sorely undervalued.

YOU ARE GORGEOUS.
Full nose, lips, and curves that for so long, society considered ugly.
Now the heiresses of oppression attempt to buy your

NATURAL BEAUTY
From a plastic surgeon.

You are intelligent: Sophia Stewart.
Mother of the Matrix.
Working to unlock the chains around our brains
As the culture creators in Hollywood sought to stake claim to the fruit of her
Advanced consciousness.

You are to be honored and elevated.
From waitresses and fast food workers, to
Professors, secretaries, and entrepreneurs.
Dusty Foot Philosophers kicking knowledge through novels, or
healing hands of medicine.
Emergency room surgeons and massage therapists.

You are not pretty for a dark-skinned girl.
You are not pretty for a light-skinned girl.
You are an unspeakable truth that defies
Eurocentric standards of beauty.

Afroed activist. Curly haired youth advocate.
Exotic dancer. Ballerina. Thermal-dynamic physicist.
English teacher.
Homeless. Drug-addicted.
Socially awkward (too eccentric).
Overlooked and not accepted, sometimes by your own people.
Remember that you are nothing less than ROYALTY.

Wife. Mother. Sister. Auntie. Friend.
Lover. Wisdom. Dreamer.
Healer. Balance. Backbone. Love.
Passion. Sadness. Anger. Joy.

Heart.
Freedom.
Black.
Queen.

Discipline

It is not easy to be a man today.

It is not easy to be a Black man today.

It is not easy to be a Black man in a foreign land due to circumstances beyond our control.

We live in a nation that sees us as strangers, but we still call it home.

Home is where the heart is.

But here, I do not see home.

Instead, I see broken households where so-called real niggaz

Shatter any illusions of real love.

Broken windows and shattered glass

Cut deeper into the soul than the window that she crashed through.

Her lacerations will heal faster than the damage done to her spirit.

Than the damage done to her daughter's innocence.

Never should a child bare witness to such callous savagery as this.

Never should a child see a man who helped raise her become a gutless coward.

These babies see us as superheroes, even if we don't.

We cannot afford to fall victim to cowardice.

It is not easy to be a man today. It is not easy to be a Black man today.

I am not a perfect man by any means.

But when push came to shove,

Her self-esteem was too low for what I perceived to be a harmless joke.

She thought putting her hands on me was somehow justified,

I found strength from somewhere deep within.
As every bit of rage swelled within me,
I could hear my mother speaking, like an emissary for God's teachings.
"Don't put your hands on nobody's daughter.
'Cause you would never want a man to put his hands on me."

It's not easy to be a man today. It is not easy to be a Black man today.
It ain't never been easy to a Black man, but imagine
What it must feel like to be a Black mans' punching bag.
Mothers. Daughters. Sisters. Friends. Lovers.
None of them have cursed us so, that we should
Ever see it as labor, to fight for and not against them.
To lift our hands in their defense, as opposed to a closed fist to
strike them down, because our egos have become too sensitive.
We are warriors. We are protectors.
We are superheroes even if we don't believe it.

So let us stand.
For the thousands of Black women who've gone missing.
Stand for those we know personally, that have been beaten down but not defeated.
Put them up on pedestals, let them rest upon their thrones,
While we become their backbones.
Be strong my brothers. We are strong my brothers.
Don't flinch. Don't give in.
Not to the vices that give us excuses.

Not to the pain, that tries to overwhelm & confuse us.

Not to arrogance;

that makes you believe your lady is a slave, and not a person.

Be a man. Be a Black man.

It's not easy, but we were made in the image of a King.

And we must rule ourselves, as he did.

With discipline fam.

With discipline.

You Are Not Invisible
~For Mary J. & the Men of Mariner's Inn.
Dedicated to the fighters. Keep fighting!

You are not invisible. I see you.
Through the haze that often covers our eyes.
Leaving us blinded. Closing our minds.

I still see you. Like I see my aunt.

She used to hustle crack cocaine for a living,
until her addiction to fast money was replaced by an
Addiction to the dope she sold.

The streets of Detroit can be ruthless and cold.
My aunt's story could've been different.
A tragedy. A rape victim.
Dead and broken. A body left somewhere outside the
Garfield Building.

But God authored a narrative worthy of witness.
She walked a path of faith and resiliency that saw her overcome.

Addiction a distant memory.
2 kids through college and now a homeowner.

The streets can be unforgiving.
This world can be a menace.
It remembers all your faults, will vilify your failures;
Dismiss your good works in an effort to forget about you.

But believe me when I say that I see you.

There's an ongoing war being waged against our people.
Black & brown bodies made ripe for target practice.
Police shoot to kill or cuff to fill quotas for
State pens & beds in private prisons.
'
The poor & homeless among us are often swept aside,
made to feel inferior.
When the Super Bowl, the Final Four, or
World Series comes to town,
They are made to seem non-existent.

These are my brothers & sisters.
YOU are my brothers & sisters.
Survivors, fighters, and unsung heroes.
The truth that nobody wants to speak of.
But I will speak up.

You are not invisible.
And you never were.
I see you.

Master Mold

There is nothing more empty than wasted time.
The precious seconds we sacrifice without merit.
Hours given way to unnecessary worries.
Minutes we can't reclaim by being in a hurry.
Fast track to nowhere (the infinite rush hour).
Hamsters contained by the wheels of the rat race.

The human becomes a machine.

An android.
An androgynous, synthetic being.
Slowly dissected like a dead insect in biology class.
Brought back to life as Frankenstein's monster, but
Not nearly as cool as Magneto.

We are tethered to our technology as if it were a leash, and
We are dogs.
Each signal emitted a whistle that bellows like an alarm.
Sends a charge through our bodies when the wrong switch is flipped.
Reducing us to docile puppies, when stout pitbull is called for.
Turning us into rabid rottweilers when we are more in need of regalness and calm.

Disoriented by mixed messages, undermined by irrational ideas;
We find ourselves at odds with our very existence.
The flesh attacks the spirit.
The want for power consumes.
The power of lust controls.
Control is never enough.

The unsatisfied hunt for more.
More knowledge, not wisdom.

More wealth, not generosity.
More humanism, not humanity.

Man meld with machine:
Transformed and reborn in the likeness of material excess & Hedonistic vanity.
Reflecting the image of darkness that emanates from false deities.
We are being programmed to prey on and be preyed upon, but not to pray.
Only to exalt the mind of man as god.

Until man can build a monument in its own image.
A walking tower of babel, testament to our descent.
And when this beast comes to life- its eyes without soul.
Piercing. Vengeful. Menacing. Cold.
We will all wonder, "where did the time go?"
As man evolves itself into oblivion,
Fallen victim to the Master Mold.

Come the Apocalypse

I share this with you as an inconvenient truth.
Not to gather acclaim. I have nothing to prove.
Fed up with living in this open air prison.
Knowing inside I'm free, but the world will tell you different.
Try to convince us we're related to a simian.
Primordial sludge, instead of divine citizens.
We were created in the image of Creator.
Great Heavenly Father, the author of all nations.

I can promise you the devil is a liar.
Deceiver by the word, and deceiver by the eye.
Moving in high places through the flesh of foul agents.
Slithering in the shadows as the world becomes snake-bitten.
In this snake pit, they plunder and pillage.
Redistribute the wealth from the dirt poor to filthy rich.

Unprecedented numbers drawing unemployment.
Military recalled for domestic deployment.
In American cities where my people are oppressed.
Tired of being hung, shot down, or beaten to death.
Gotta separate what's real from their satanic rituals
Divide and conquer ops played by agent provocateurs.

People so afraid of death, they are scared to live.
Petrified by a well-advertised flu virus.
Of course we mourn for the people we lost.
But it's a disservice if we don't question it all.
As symbolism manifests into mysticism,
People yelling out they can't breathe.
Now they're suffocating.
From ventilators, or tear gas canisters blasted at protestors,

Choking behind a mask.

Fire and bullets fly from here to Yemen & Gaza
Non-violent offenders still suffer in lockup.
Authoritarian nations expand their surveillance.
Control what you think and speak, credit to Facebook.
Skynet unleashed to keep the masses in line.
Put drones over your city just for being outside.
Weaponized even further when you're speaking your mind.
We are prisoners of thought in the war of our times.
As the Apocalypse comes with a needle & gun.
The Apocalypse comes with a needle & gun.

The Resonance of Silent Weapons

Does the revolution begin before or after the unholy war?
It seems that mankind has no qualms with marching itself off a cliff.
Boastful, narcissistic, and indignant,
Yet ill-equipped to face the extent of its fears.

Mankind.

Gerbils chasing their tails inside a cage without bars.
Spiritual beings being sucked dry of their souls.
Exhausted by the relentless fight to transform a demonic system into a less
Ungodly one.

Indeed, I do yearn to realize the fullness of freedom, to
See a just world in my lifetime,
But I do not put much stock in fairytales.

This world was in disarray long before I was born.
It might still be in chaos long after I'm gone.
Nevertheless, I find awe in the splendor that is the human experience.

A child born without words to speak, will come to master several languages.
A child without understanding of science and arithmetic will grow up to be a renowned scholar & mathematician.

A little boy and girl who play on the playground everyday will
give each other their first scars.
Push one another off the swings at the park,
Despise each other in high school, and
Fall in love before they graduate college.

Mankind. This is our story.

Unfortunately, there are powers that exist on this
Earth with grand designs on how the book should be written:
Authors of pain, whose craft is to construct a narrative that suggests
Going over the cliff is your bridge to enlightenment, when they
Know damn well it was always a road to nowhere.
It is not a coincidence that
Ghettos exist in every corner of the Earth.
It is not by accident that masses of people are
Pushed to their limits almost simultaneously, and shortly thereafter
Rivers of blood flood the streets like
Ocean waves disturbed by hurricanes.
We have entered some turbulent waters.

Mankind.

Divided and conquered by false archetypes.
Hoods across America look like nations hit by its bombs.
Economic hitmen redistribute the resources from poor to rich.
Too often, those poor faces look eerily familiar.

Our cities are patrolled by trained killers.
Our schools are run like failed businesses.
Our land, our culture, even our bodies are up for sale to the
Highest bidder.

There is no left or right.
Power chooses its own side.

Mankind.

We are the survivors of government sanctioned genocide.
We are the subjects of psychological operations funded by

Major corporations, non-governmental organizations, and
Philanthropic foundations.

Ford. Rockefeller. Rothschild. Gates.
The names have not changed, and neither has the game.

Create dissension, stir the public's interest.
Steer the agenda. Present a resolution to complete their initiative.

Mankind.

Don't be fooled by the news.

Mankind.

Think for yourself.

Mankind.

You are not alone.

Mankind.

Please listen. Stay prayerful.

Beware the resonance of silent weapons.
Beware the resonance of silent weapons.

Remember that the story to be written is still ours.

Endure

~Dedicated to our youth facing war in all its forms. May your light endure.

Sometimes the world is ugly, like when
Children are robbed of their childhood.
When the roar of laughter and games falls silent,
As the raucous booms of bombs echoes through the atmosphere.
Life is not always sweet.
We shed tears for our loved ones that have fallen,
But the violence does not slack as we cry for peace.

There are moments where we are left with nothing more than
Questions without sufficient answers.
Speechless.
Silent.
Cold.
Numbed by the vibrations of a hateful world,
Shaking humankind to its core.
The fault lines we disturb so often,
Cause more devastation than the worst of earthquakes.
Perhaps, man is the most dangerous of natural disasters.

Still, there shines a light, however dim.
A brightness that flickers on occasion, to remind us that
We are soulful beings.
Take a heavy breath, exhale.
Feel your heart beating.
Still here.

We are alive for a purpose beyond logic and reason.
The trials of faith, that test our resiliency,
Bringing our beliefs under examination
Pushing us to discover sufficient answers for

Questions we haven't thought to ask.

Bear witness to the child whose smile brings sunlight to a room.
Despite the horrors she has seen, as her mother was persecuted.
Bless the son, who kept his soul amidst the bedlam faced in war.
Wipes the tears from sister's eyes,
They are their parents' pride & joy.

Sometimes the world can be ugly.
But we would be remiss not to recognize its majesty.
Birds arranging boisterous tunes that herald daybreak,
Mimicking the joys of life outside the chaos.
Sweet indeed.

My favorite things are memories of yesterday,
Sparked by melodies from Coltrane.
Catching passes and shooting baskets,
Chasing girls around the neighborhood, playing tag.

Before the veil was lifted.
Before innocence was lost.
An accidental shooting.
A stabbing over drugs (or pride).
Before the towers were vaporized and
We descended into endless conflict,
There was life.

Not always sweet, but worth living.
Even as handcuffs choked my wrists for a crime
I didn't commit.
Accused of stealing.
Even as poverty and debt,
Attempt to suffocate any remnants of greatness that

Burn within.
I embrace all of it.

Unshaken in my trust of the Creator,
Despite my frustrations.
I still believe that one day I will catch my queen (tag).
And we shall
Serve our people.
Bringing smiles to kids who never found their childhood.
Reconnecting with an innocence lost,
A flickering light that becomes a flame and endures.

When the Music Stops

Will you be there when the music stops?
After our wounds and scars are exposed to the light, where
there is nowhere to escape, no place to hide.
I imagine you, beautiful and brilliant.
Faithful, yet flawed because anything more is unrealistic.

> But when the honeymoon sets for a bold sunrise;
> For those bitter cold winters.
> For that everyday grind.
> Can we still dance the night away, under a brisk autumn rain?
> Share our love & war stories,
> Blessed joys & cursed pain.

> If so, then let us move in unison.
> Let us groove to African rhythms.
> Get Caribbean dancehall sweaty
> Before we jit to drum patterns and house mixes mastered
> For ghettotech classics.
> Let our steps become a melody to give thanks for our existence.
> Let our movements be a tribute to the ancestors who rest, but walk with us.

I cannot promise you the world.

Neither the stars, nor riches.

I can only promise to give you a genuine love that is unconditional.

I will fight for you.

Ashy knuckles cracked and bloody if needed.

Be at your bedside when you're sick,

to nurse you back to health.

No picket fences, but forehead kisses to mend the

brokenhearted memories of relationships past.

Together we will co-write ballads, that would make

Jill Scott & Aaliyah blush.

Rock the boat until it CAPSIZES, as

I submerge myself in your waters until

This sacred baptism produces new life.

I can't promise you the world.

Neither the stars, nor riches.

I can only promise to give you a genuine love that is unconditional.

I will not fight you.

I'm not one to argue. I can't stand to raise my voice.

On the days that we disagree, can we handle it respectfully?

There might be days where you can't stand me.

I understand, but do no put your hands on me,

'Cause I will not raise a hand toward you.

Break up to make up, is a game for fools that we will not play.

I will give you space. I will let you breathe.

But you will not go to sleep being mad at me.

So, after we've toasted *cherry wine* to Nas and Amy Winehouse.

Reminisced on high school dances and college house parties getting loose to *Godzilla*

Listened to Charity, sharing *beautiful moments* that Nat King Cole would simply describe as *unforgettable*.

After last call & the DJ has played the last song.

I'll be standing right here, when the music stops.

Just waiting, to take your hand.

To Love a Stranger from Afar

~For Alexandra Tracy (Inspired by the song "So Easy" by Phylicia Ashley Barron)
*In Memory of Phylicia Ashley Barron. A beloved musician, a beautiful woman, and incredible spirit whom I only got to know through her music. May the joy & grace of the Most High be with you & your loved ones.

Am I wrong to love a stranger from afar?
If so, then I embrace my penance willingly.
Let my eyes flow freely with
Tears of joy, and those of sorrow.
Thankful for glorious todays, as I
Grieve for lost tomorrows.

I could hear her soul speaking to me.
She of Afro-Latina splendor,
San Diego sunlight shining,
California dreams, whispering a sultry melody.
She sang the sweetest threat,
I'd ever heard before:
"Don't fall in love with me, or
I'll just have to love you more"

Her beauty resonated from within.
A gifted songstress, whose ballads spoke of
True love that too often goes unrealized.
Perhaps, she was not of this Earth.
I believe she was a guardian angel
Only meant to share a glimpse of her radiance,
Enough to remind of us that the Creator exists.

You were never meant to suffer.
Never meant to live in such an ugly world as this.
I am saddened, but gracious.

Saddened that our paths never crossed,
Gracious that I got to hear your voice.
Humbled by the beat of your heart, gifted to my ears as the
Healing sound of undying bliss.
A melody from Heaven,
Both sultry and sacred.
I'll be waiting for you, right across the street,
Among the many who love you, because
You made it so easy.

After Mourning
~In Memory of Atatiana Jefferson & her father, Marquis

Atatiana Jefferson will not be the last.
But she should be.
Atatiana Jefferson will not be the last.
But she should be.

She should be playing video games with her nephew this weekend.
Instead her family plans funeral arrangements.

Brothers & sisters come together, once again.
In outrage.
In protest.
We cry out to the heavens for justice as
 Another light cast too brightly for the darkness of this world is
Dimmed to an uneasy sunset.

I do not have the words to ease the pain of her parents.
I do not have the words to quiet the unsettled fear and anger of her loved ones.
I cannot erase the sadness & tears that have become far too common.
We do this dance far too often.
So, I can only say I love you.
And stand by it.

The work continues today, and for every tomorrow we are gifted.
Celebrate the life Atatiana lived.
Breathe in and exhale every bit of emotion you feel.

Do not mask your passion.
It is real.
Do not suppress your anger.
It is real.

Be a whole, free human being as God intended.
Make no apologies for the skin you were given.

Embrace the reality that you might do nothing wrong, and in your innocence,
Fall victim to a coward's gun.

Especially if the shooter is white.
And granted a license to kill with a badge & a uniform.
I can only say I love you, and stand by it.

In love, I do not call for violence.
But we have reached the point where diplomacy must be fortified by self-defense.

I am fed up with my people's suffering.
I am fed up with America's disregard for our humanity.
I am fed up with America in totality.

Aaron Dean lives.
Atatiana Jefferson is no longer here.
Aaron Dean was charged with murder.
He may or may not go to prison.
Atatiana Jefferson is no longer here.

I can only say I love you, and stand by it.

Aiyana Stanley-Jones.
Sandra Bland.
Rekia Boyd.
Charleena Lyles.
Atatiana Jefferson.

Remember their names.

Tell their stories.

After outrage.
After sadness.
After mourning.
Look at our sisters.
Say I love you.

Stand by it.

Oasis

Give me freedom, or
I will seek the tools to defend myself.
I do not court death, yet
I will not live under your illusions of peace, that
Masquerade behind the guise of order.

Our street corners are still a notorious a place, but
Not nearly as wicked as what festers in the hearts of
Immoral men that put assault weapons in our neighborhoods.
Those that send broken kids to boot camp,
Strip them of any semblance of independence.
Transform them into weapons of mass destruction,
Deploy them to desert battlefields that mimic the urban jungles they come from.

My people have no business in your uniforms.

Not for lack of patriotism or bravery.
Black men and women have
Sacrificed themselves far too often in the service of
America.

My people have no business in your uniforms.

Not for lack of skill or intellect.
From the Buffalo Soldiers to the Tuskegee Airmen,
My people have been instrumental in deciding the outcome of
America's ongoing beef with the world at-large.

We have no business in your uniforms, because
No matter how valiantly we serve,
What we receive in return, is akin to

A set of bounced checks.
A condescending pat on the head.
A cop's clip emptied into a pregnant mother,
A cop's chokehold siphoning a father's last breath.

We wear the suit and tie,
Don the camouflage fatigues,
Sport the shield like a cape and cowl.
But in the end, our backs remain broken.
We have carried the bane of you for far too long,
America.

Poison to the veins,
A venomous relationship.
We've been mortal enemies since the days of colonies, when the
United States was merely a rotten seed in
Great Britain's limp dick.

We have no business in your uniforms.
We have no business being a party to the violence you've wrought.
The violence that leaves nations desolate and starving.
The violence that leaves our neighbors, friends, and family members
Stifled with illness.
We have not forgotten Flint, Rick Snyder.

Your water is unclean.
It is toxic to us.
We are dying of thirst.
We are dying of thirst.
Unable to locate the oasis, slowly drowning in quicksand.

Masquerade

I've grown tired of listening to symphonies of destruction.
Broken strings shrieking like Freddy Krueger's claws
Scraping against a weathered chalkboard in fluctuating minor keys.
Reckless staccato drums heralding discord, blare through the speakers of
Enchanted zombies that seemingly fail to notice.
So consumed with empty debates, they
Spit in the face of educated discourse.
People have become so offended by different points of view, that
They would prefer isolation swallow them whole,
As opposed to cultivating relationships that don't conform to the
psychosis of new normals.

An age of loose morals where
Pop culture icons have become low-tier deities for a
Line of *apprentices* initiated into the
Mysteries of idol worship.
Rituals of egoistic paternalism permeate every facet of society.
Methods of mass conditioning designed to strip men & women of
Critical thought and free will have become religion.
A doctrine of power and control that manifests as entitlement.
A notion that title is akin to righteousness.
Deceived by arrogance, the people now aspire to godhood.
But find themselves mired in the crux of fear.
A crucible aptly suited for wayward mortals.

These are the days of the masquerade.
Where false kings are crowned as the crowds parade.
Where false queens disguise what's behind their faces.
But their motives are revealed by the masks they embrace.
A lost generation that fails to question everything except our Creator.
Obsessed with occupying a seat at the enemy's table.

Brothers and sisters convinced that freedom is found in acquiescence.
They wear the mask to fit in.
Others fulfill their roles as performing activists
Ready to jump at the sound of every dog whistle.
Sleight is mastered by the invisible hand.
As the master plan hides in plain sight.
And the truth disappears into nothingness.

The masquerade. A dance with the devil.
A ball for self-professed luminaries engulfed by the
Seduction of duality.
Black & white paradigms used to conceal the
Culling of mankind through clandestine crimes.
A left-right goose step to orchestrate compliance.
The world finds itself in the crosshairs of professional liars lurking as wolves.
Mercenaries well-compensated to pull wool over the eyes of sheep.
Set the table for their guests and feast.
A system designed in the image of the beast.

Contact tracing? Digital surveillance.
Shutdown announced? Martial law already in place.
Misdiagnosis. Victims of malpractice.
Doctors with incentive to push pandemic panic.
Skeptics suppressed. Those who press further fired.
Medical journals publish, but pull the contrary science.
Cops are still shooting at us on behalf of looters:
Corporations eating while mom & pops getting booted.
Elders dying alone 'cause a visit is not permitted.
Decisions being made on your behalf without permission.
Liquor store open next door to a McDonald's, where a
Chain smoker puts on a mask to fight corona.
Injuries and death tolls counted after a mushroom cloud is seen
Following an explosion in Beirut,

Attributed to fireworks.

The masquerade.
Symphonies of destruction.
The masquerade.
A dance with the devil.
The masquerade.
A crowning of false kings & queens engulfed by the seduction of duality.
Black & white paradigms become casualties hued red & blue.
Organized chaos (orchestrated compliance).
We suffocate.
And we bleed.

Call & Response (By the Blind No More)

Sometimes I wonder if we are living in the last days, or
Simply unfortunate witnesses to the prelude.
Today is an unpleasant age.
An era rife with boundless falsehoods
Aimed at casting binds upon the feet of free thinkers to slow their
March toward paradise.
Unfit rulers play wicked games with the lives of
unwitting subjects who've been subjugated to a condition of subservience.
Submission to agendas without substance.
Charmed by the subversive philosophies of
Sub-human wretches whose blasphemous ideals have convinced the world to substitute
Unworthy men & women as surrogates for the true and living God.

I've grown impatient, as I
Watch the world burn slowly.
The powers of this Earth sit comfortably in shadows like
Cowardly comic book villains,
Unable to square up and fight their wars themselves.
They send in agents of their cabals.
Brainwashed, ego-driven, mindless drones that
Go out to slaughter countless people
With a ready-made excuse of simply following orders.

Our brothers and sisters bleed,
As appeals for justice fall upon deaf ears. Of course,
I find it absurd to plead with our enemies for freedom
That our beloved Creator already gave us from the moment
We were conceived in the womb.
Protestors flood the streets screaming, "Black Lives Matter!"
And I ask my people, who are we appealing to?
Such a minor valuation placed on our existence,

As if we need to prove that we are human beings.
As if we need to prove we should be treated humanely.

Black Lives Matter.

A refrain that has only proven to separate the overt racists from the
Clandestine ones.
A chorus for covert operations
Disguised as a righteous war cry for revolution.
Symbols of oppression are pulled to the ground, to
Lay the foundation for future fascism packaged as progress.
Buildings burn in the night as sigils signaling the demise of
America's divided states.
Old world doctrines give way to new age mantras
Whilst a new world order emerges through old school chaos.
Modern warfare: black ops.
Target in the crosshairs of undercover operatives
Staging anarchy at a heartland Autozone
While ambiguous agitators claim victory,
As Seattle concedes a portion of the city as an autonomous zone (for a limited time only).

Only until police abandon their illusions of humility,
Like precincts left behind to serve as kindling
For fires ignited by a convergence of repressive state violence and
Mystical alchemy applied through occult science.
Current events have not emerged by happenstance.
These rapids become more tumultuous with every shooting,
With every beating.
Every time a citizen or activist is snatched off the street, and pulled
Through a smashed car window from a vehicle surrounded by
Recreants with a license to commit acts of treason.
Under the watch of federal agents overseeing military operations,

With orders from the present court jester-in-chief,
These disgusting thugs produce hell on Earth with the vigor of
Pseudo minutemen raising their muskets to Make America Great Again.
A mythological idiom that boasts a nation of liberty & justice.
A baseless fallacy of revisionist history.
Fiction masquerading as a fantastic fairytale.
A dream that will never be realized.

Make America Great Again.

A refrain that has only proven to separate the overt racists from the
Clandestine ones.
A chorus for covert operations
Disguised as a righteous war cry for revolution.
Symbols of oppression resurfacing to
Lay the foundation for future fascism packaged as patriotism.
21st Century lynchings executed by Manchurian henchmen.
Teenage assassins raised by the cult of white supremacy,
Blast at church goers and assassinate dissidents that condemn America for its
Crimes against my kinfolk.
Strange fruit swinging from southern trees ruled suicide.
Black beauty found dead in a jail cell ruled suicide.
Young soldier shot by Detroit Police execution style (deemed justified).

Talking heads politicize left-right paradigms.
Initiated satanists puppeteer and weaponize
Figureheads with tattered false flags on both sides.
Redneck druids and Boulé negroes
Sold to the masses as American heroes.
Theater of civil war being brought to our doorsteps
But not before the climax of the present antebellum.

Worldwide deception.

Collapse of America.
Faux revolutionaries and
Synthetic patriots
Give away their freedom in exchange for being safe
A yoke and a muzzle (they are terrified of each other).
A vaccine and a shovel (they are terrified of each other).
But change gon' come if we vote in the next election?

Insult to my intelligence.
Disgusted by their rhetoric.
When will the people get tired and say, "enough of this"?
Maybe never (But I'm praying for us).
Stop living in fear (Start praying for us).
Armed in mind, body, and soul.
Prepared to answer the call of the Holy One.
Ready to respond in faith.
Cut the heads off of treacherous snakes.
Living in freedom, and not fear.
Ruled by the blind no more.

The Watchman's Opus

These verses aren't written for hollow recognition.
This gift, the art of language, serves as a hammer & nail.
A sword & shield.
Tools to construct a future with the audacity to defy the delusions that the
Human race has been subjected to.
Weapons of spiritual warfare forged through rhymes that hope to emulate
The wisdom of parables found in the holy scriptures.
I am not flawless by any measure.
Nonetheless, I pursue perfection.
Praying to be reshaped and molded as righteous clay.
Reconstructed from a simple man, to a living fortress built to serve those who
Find it difficult to stand.

I am a man of faith, though there are days that the evil of this world
Seems to have its way.
Enraged by the hatred that prevails in our society,
I find myself itching to unleash wrathful vengeance against those that bring harm to my people.
I find myself preoccupied too often with a relentless barrage of images that
Perpetuate lawlessness.
Sex & violence amplified to fever pitch.
Frequencies of discontent that manifest as abhorrent sickness.

I cannot stand indifferently.
There must be a witness to the wretchedness we have allowed to persist.
American ghettos painted red with the blood of innocents gunned down
By wannabe gangsters.
From parasites with badges, to slave minded savages imitating wack rappers

Who emulate mafioso grandstanding.
Rat bastards that brutalize our communities
But won't wage war against the lackeys of the oppressor class.
Born queens forfeiting their crowns & kingdoms in exchange for fans only interested in sensual thots as opposed to critical thoughts.
Sex & violence amplified to fever pitch.
Thousands of women and children disappearing, seemingly into a vortex.
Trafficking. Enslavement.
International black market business booming with protection
From state and corporate interests.
Frequencies of discontent that manifest as abhorrent sickness.
ICE detention centers filled with men, women, and children stripped of their dignity.
Inhumanity established as common practice.
Families destroyed.
Torture realizing its purpose, transcending form.
Echoes of Guantanamo Bay & Mongola State Prison.
Alcatraz Island & Abu Ghraib.
Prisoners at Clinton Correctional Facility
Abused by guards under threat and orders issued by a coward named
Andrew Cuomo.
It is no coincidence that he was so quick to
Put the citizenry of New York under
Lockdown.
No coincidence that he advocates for cowering behind a mask.
Symbolic language for coded conversations.

Powerful puppets playing dress-up games.
Donald Trump making out with a treasonous hag.
Rudy Guiliani dressed in drag
Policies of stop and frisk take on greater significance,

when viewed through the lens of private retreats and initiation rituals.
Sacrificial lambs made of human beings
As three buildings collapsed at the World Trade Center in 2001.
A story sold to citizens on the premise of patriotism and self-defense.
In reality, an orchestrated event used as the impetus for an unholy war.
A relentless barrage of images that perpetuate lawlessness.

America moves closer to the end of its empire.
Going the way of Rome & Greece,
But will it actually cede power, or simply rebrand itself as
A world monolith in further devotion to the mysteries of the beast?
Hegemon. Leviathan.
A corporation that doubles as a nation state,
Portraying the role of Babylon for the modern age.
The world at-large slips further into slumber,
Mislead by the example of dictators, oligarchs, moguls, and eugenicists.
Elitists pretending to serve the masses as honorable visionaries and philanthropists.
Operating in plain sight as ventriloquists manipulating human action & consciousness.
I cannot stand indifferently.

The people feed upon crumbs, or eat each other.
Chasing the blinding radiance of limelight,
Man becomes monkey performing acrobatics to fulfill the twisted fantasies of ringmasters.
Stone hearted reptiles with cold ambition.
Pied pipers hypnotizing the populace to baptize them into the society of bread and circuses.
We have become voyeurs of spectacle.
Actors in the theater of the absurd.

The time is too urgent for petty disagreements, fruitless gossip, and blind allegiance to a System that authorizes your demise as they whitewash your dashikis.
Kneel for false kings.
Put our elders in nursing homes to rot, let them die alone.
Sport the Cartier Buffs for street cred.
And implore you to stay at home.
Stay in your place.
Not question the authority or motivation of the so-called illuminated.

Today beckons more than childish compliance to draconian rules.
Today beckons more than defeatist conformity to the new abnormal.
Where is the soul of man?
Find yours.
Where is the faith of the saints?
Find yours.
Be vigilant. Stand guard.
Mind yours.
Keep watch.
Seek the truth and live it (my opus).
Write yours.

Play My Music Loud

Play my music loud.
Let it bang through your speakers.
Shake the foundation of these old city streets.
Hear me when I sing you a song for my people.
Prayers to the Father,
and a message to my enemies.

I do not fear the uncertainty of today.
I implore you to be fearless as well.
We are all imperfect beings living on borrowed time (in this realm).
We might as well be free.
Not reckless or ratchet.
Not foolish or arrogant.
Just free.
In tune with the best versions of ourselves, to offset the distorted notes that seek to
Undermine our future.
Turn up the volume to a level that pays respects to Radio Raheem.
Boombox blasting, playing old school classics that make you think about
The Funk Brothers and the boom-bap.
Takes you back to the lunch table cyphers.
Drumsticks made out of pencils & pop bottles, as emcees spit sixteens over the
Grinding beat.
We have to find that vibe again.
'Clipse the glass ceilings put in place to set limits on our imagination
(our aptitude for greatness).
Snap the handcuffs and ball & chain that tries to weigh us down,
As those who move in darkness attempt to drown us.

I've been through struggle & pain.
Hospital stay caused by an enzyme imbalance in my kidneys.
Preceded by an out of body experience.
Struggling to rest.
Wrestling with spirit.
Intricate thoughts unfiltered.
Misdiagnosed with a behavioral condition.
Had to check the doctor for disrespect toward Mama.
He sent in his pale-faced witch (nurse) flanked by two raccoons in uniform.
To ensure that I took an unnecessary dose of medication.
The first & last time my health will be left in the hands of devils.
I am a man of peace.
But if forced to war,
I will not concede my life to spare another who seeks my downfall
(will defend me & mine at all costs).
May those that encroach my freedom & yours suffer for their crimes.
Deep breath. Fall back.
Vengeance is the Lord's.

Play my music loud.
Let it bang through your speakers.
Shake the foundation of these old city streets.
Hear me when I sing you a song for my people.
Prayers to the Father,
And a message to my enemies.

We come from proud and resilient people.
But I see too much pride today, not enough resiliency.
Senseless bickering driven by internet gossip.
Difference of opinion?

Twitter fingers.
Shots fired.
Paragons of virtue signaling set the tone of fascism.
Vultures lurk for the bones of those "cancelled."
How long before the words I speak shock and offend you?
Before you forget the days I love and defend you?
Difficult to understand the psyche of my sistas.
Emblems of a generation living in its feelings.
Everything's reactionary.
People hardly listen.
Brothas ain't exempt.
They can be the worst offenders.
Division in the homes.
Our community, exposed.
Embodying an image of us we don't control.
Tethered to the rhetoric of Hollywood celebrities.
Academic narratives that don't respect the projects.
We've become the product of social engineering.
Coordinated efforts to destroy the holy temples.
Men & women separated.
Fabricated hatred.
Women unprotected. Men incarcerated.
Roles get conflated through trauma that's unstated.
Child molestation, rape, and castration.
Savages produced by the scars of buck breaking.
Bad girls showing their ass for liberation,
Scream independence in tears.
Fearing abuse (and abandonment).
A legacy of unresolved pain,
But we gon' need each other if conditions gon' change.

Tear each other down, we'll be in the same place.
Rowing upstream against open floodgates

Play my music loud.
Let it bang through your speakers.
Shake the foundation of these old city streets.
Hear me when I sing you a song for my people.
Prayers to the Father,
and a message to my enemies.

I will not go quietly into the night (put hands on those who encroach my freedom).
I hope that you will commit to the fight as well.
Find the joy this world tries to convince us no longer exists.
Hold onto it the way champions embrace their trophies.
Hold onto it like parents cradling their newborns.
Like man & wife engaged in passionate embrace after too much time apart.
Joy is an extension of our faith.
Music to the ears of the saints, though to me it might sound like a breakbeat.
DJ Diztracted scratching at the family barbecue.
The Cypher kicking freestyles on the Diag.
Michigan Band playing "The Victors"
After touchdowns.
Shoes squeaking across gymnasium floors.
Helping to clean Cliff Keen & Crisler Arena.
Keeping focused on rhymes written with purpose.
Fighting obstacles knowing us is stronger than I.
Absent of perspective & distance,
I have love for all my family ties.
Bloodlines rich in resistance.
Southern hospitality & toughness instilled by

Jim Crow-era Mississippians.
Legacy of an abolitionist in my veins.
Detroit roots heavy.
I am William Lambert's kinfolk.
My soul expressed through poems that speak of underground Hip-Hop and
Underground Railroad.
The fight I speak of is one to hear the sound of heavenly music.
Beautiful babies raised to know God.
Not living with the fear of those who've come before,
Only with their strength & their love.

The sound of heavenly music.
Black folks free to dance in peace,
But well-prepared for what's to come.
Protect your sisters (and your brothers), but do not play the fool for anyone.

The sound of heavenly music.
Veils lifted from our eyes.
Ears unplugged to hear the voice of wisdom more clearly.
Deep, authentic laughter made familiar once again.
Shedding of tears to honor those unable to share their laughs with us.

Play my music loud.
A harp & trumpet with accompaniment from
Bass guitar, grand piano, and 808 drum.
Joy. Hope. Wisdom. Fight. Freedom. Faith.
Featuring
Soul & Funk.

www.ingramcontent.com/pod-product-compliance
Lightning Source LLC
Chambersburg PA
CBHW022016160426
43197CB00007B/454